Documenta 11

Matthew Arnatt & Matthew Collings

Artwords Press 2002

Documenta 11
Matthew Arnatt and Matthew Collings

**ARTWORDSPR
ESS**

Published by Artwords Press
65a Rivington Street
London EC2A 3QQ
www.artwords.co.uk

Design: Secondary Modern
Printed by Aldgate Press

ISBN 0-9543908-0-6

Documenta 11

... An 'at home' with English Italianate middle-class painting to tell the truth. And I like cross-eyed girls with high tone. Slight Alexander Cousins' feel to blocky backdrops - fine, kissable hands. Transparent. Antidote to the outrageous sentimentality of Documenta11, which I enjoyed.
Matthew Arnatt

OK I'll go and see the Romney show. Tell me more about your responses to Documenta. I found the sentimentality depressing.
Matthew Collings

I don't understand what the difference is between watching an Eskimo instruct another Eskimo on skinning a seal and people seeing you teach me how to gut an artist; beyond the potential for brute inapplicability. Same audience (discounting niceties like size and sophistication of stomach). Otherwise, what are the non–Bambi relations of 'believability' as not falsely determined within this partial showlike context? And are Eskimos patronising? Or bad at gutting? Why not weight the Eskimos more? Heavy them up a bit? (Monitors were all ranged at pub height near exits). Have I been, without knowing it, documenting precisely the remedial condition of guilty self-centred self-consciousness that one takes to be the self-correcting condition of one's culpable friends always anyway? It's just that I'm unwatchable?

Despite and including morbidity, things to enjoy. Not Dieter Rot or A Sepia Falling Indian. But all the installation looked dated and didactic (always did) ... liked Eskimos, Hanne Darboven films, all the films about workers and film about lean Congolese sex-education (an eye-opener for me). Really enjoyed early 70s film about Palestinian refugees. Best thing I liked? Rwandan genocide film with radio excerpts, because it was stunning. *MA*

Wow, you noticed a lot of things I didn't. I remember a film of a room that looked like an exhibition space for a warehouse show in London circa early 90s, which had a soundtrack of moaning or something, that might have been the lingering ghostly aftermath of tortures or genocide. Was that the Rwandan film?
  The Eskimo films were fine. That stuff is good. Only they would be better on TV, because you could lie on the sofa and watch them. Ha ha, yes, that's true, it would be good to make the non tie-up between vegetarianism and Eskimos. I liked Steve McQueen's film about the gold miners. Did you see it? He had another one, too, set in the Caribbean, which was a mess. Well, I don't know about Hanne Darboven. I can't bear to keep seeing those crossed out numbers. What was her film?
MC

No, your rather elegant and reductive target paintings would have been distasteful in the Rwandan film. Maggie told me to go back in and see the McQueen – I was feeling purged and

bitter. The other, that you mention, had the
dropping Carib Indians and tinted waves. Little
Darboven films were black and white shaky-cam
interiors, but unexpected cluttered antiquarian
interiors - somehow had a 'Blow-Up' feel, or
even the gun-maker's in Genoa in the 'Day of the
Jackal'. (Still with targets)!
  Yep, crappy old TV wins hands-down everytime.
Probably all these things are for people who just
don't understand TV - a bit like Japanese WWII
soldiers isolated on islands fighting forgotten
battles. Erect people who believe that some kind
of moral self-determination is advisable. Lookout!
Here comes an unusually thoughtful and sensitive
Lee Marvin ...
  I was interested in Allan Sekula ('Fish Story') -
what did you think? Though mostly I thought the
older and 'conceptual' artists met another poorly
bracketed end, don't you agree? So you are right,
something like that cleverly positioned 'Neue-
BANK' painting you showed at Milton Keynes
would have been extremely good and a lesson in
controlling upon the nose, and gruellingly
'flipping', contrivances - to curators. No?
MA

I don't know what that fish film is. No, didn't see
the Darboven films.
MC

By the way, I thought Giuseppe Gabellone,
artificial flowers, chucked in with Yinka
Shonibare; was good. Definitely not one of those
artists who liked to wear hard-hats - to dancingly

scrape-off and quarantine realism. Not like Sekula
(who incidentally gave me an undissolved E.A.
Poeish Northern Atlantic nightmare - skinnily
distended 80s artists with ancient pencil thin
erections, lashed to the mast of the *S. S. Arnolfini* -
and me, naked on an ice-floe, luminous in the
Arctic day-night, trembling).

So it's easy to see how someone like this
Giuseppe (who's about thirty?) evades so
graciously - that generation's snagged self-
consciousnesses; and incidentally quickly scales
the kind of reflexivity or back-to-frontness that
they all so dryly birthed, and shelled, and never
gave up.

He doesn't do that, he does something sharper,
but you could say that he did - and it wouldn't be
weird. Well it would be really. But who talks
about content? Cerith does. Pinned-up alongside
himself; so as to look at, that is.
MA

I didn't notice Giuseppe - describe the things
more. I thought this was the first time I didn't
find Y. Shonibare totally boring. It had a bit of
theatrical comic presence. Cerith's thing was the
usual light (as in not substantial, without presence)
formalism you find everywhere; could have been
Fareed Armali or someone like that, dragging on
from the 80s. Anyway I was surprised how good
Steve McQueen's film was. I tried praising it to
some obedient zombies (obeying the invisible
forces that drive art-wraiths) in the art critics'
dorm I was staying in in Kassel, and they sneered,
saying McQueen is usually playful but this was

conventional and he was trying too hard, so I
stopped that.
  What about this Gabelloni?
MC

> I liked G. Gabellone – Bluish Flowers – constructs
> – large photographic prints behind glass. But I
> liked most of the post-glacial photography. But I
> asked you about a couple of things: Sekula for
> instance, and yes I liked the Inuit films and most
> of the smallish-serious documentary-styled films –
> but that's just the endless sublimation of my
> interests to dulled taste – economy of expression –
> pocketable – something like that. I'm hoping that
> you don't believe in these conjunctions as they
> appear: phantoms of infant categorizations. Wasn't
> most of the film a bit BBC early 90s? (You know
> about these things). I think Cerith would be fine
> – in a crumbling Curly-Wurly mid-90s way –
> apart from the punctiliousness that creeps in.
> Sweet and thin only partially very nice. Were
> those zombies critics?
> *MA*

What film are you saying was BBC early 90s?
That's an incredibly sophisticated nuance of a
category. The mirror ball in Cerith refers to the
mid-90s I suppose: that moment's sudden mass
taste for retro-60s and retro-70s. But the
anything-goes expanded consciousness
conceptualism is the thing I meant that is
dragging on from the 80s. I mean post Neo Geo,
where Eco replaces Geo, not Umberto but
naturephilia. And with that an all-encompassing

do-goodingness that leads to a generally accepted
idea, in the 90s, while YBAs are underway (and
even slightly overlapping with YBAs) that certain
broken-down or broken-up ways of thinking that
have come about, must necessarily have literally
broken-up types of art to match. Broken-upness is
now magically sophisticated. In fact logically one
thing doesn't necessarily lead to the other. You
ask about the zombies: they were critics and
curators, maybe artists and writers. It was a
converted factory, near the Brewery place, which
some art people had kindly made into a dorm for
critics. It cost very little to stay there. Nothing for
me actually since I left without paying, like
Dustin Hoffman stealing the sandwiches which
were free anyway, at the hipsters' party in
Midnight Cowboy - it was pretty sick of me! I
think the dorm may even have been art of some
kind. I was literally benefiting from it by staying
there - literally benefiting from Documenta-style
art concepts. I went round the various parts of
Documenta over the next two days, including the
press conference, really down, returning to my
bunk in the evenings. I couldn't stand going into
room after room in the various exhibition spaces,
and seeing what I later remembered as endless
piles of charred twigs with gospel music playing.
Actually when I analysed this fantasy memory it
was really one particular pile of old bits of cars,
from South Africa, maybe, made into a visually
horrible sculpture thing, which really did have
gospel music playing. And everyone on the
platform - I think there were about 12 sub-
curators as well as the main guy, weren't there? -

at the press conference, was pulling pious faces
and feeling the pain of suffering, or suffering pain,
or at least mincing and wincing a lot. I think I
generated the charred twigs fantasy from the
hand-out poster I picked up at the press
conference, showing Thomas Hirschhorn's
Monument to Bataille, which turned out to be a
big hit at the Documenta, and explaining
Hirschhorn's deep thinking about the
Monument. Previous Monuments - including one
to Spinoza, I think - were illustrated, and they all
looked like Guy Fawkes.
MC

The thing about broken-up is that it assumes,
rather blandly, that things were ever composed. So
that the involved dichotomies endlessly service
master tropes congenially attaching to our
appreciations. And things remain horribly
Wodehousian - especially in their formidable
domesticity, i.e. everyone 'Knows' on the basis of
an inverted gnosis - something like a principled
snobbery - that employs into 'service' the
creatures of Africa (richly coloured and dancing
given half-a-chance), and the tortured
'sensibilities' of the geographically distanced
victims of political and economic 'atrocity' - and
uniforms them. In that way - the centre's apology
for its own centrality - draws into its own hideous
and kinky household, with the relish of a Mrs
Beaton, the exotic fruit of otherness, and pounds
it into a jelly; disgusting. Actually my mother
made jellies by leaving fruit in tights dripping into
buckets - very Annette Messager. Otherwise I

have a slight problem with you as the impious 'Amadeus' ingrate, we ordinary mortals just queued for our films.

But back to BBC, there was a period when self-consciousness first struck the BBC – which (recall, I don't know what I'm talking about), had been largely dowdy/psychedelic; a bit like your own presentation of your youth. Those first tentative and awkward gestures towards 'accountability' were best understood in terms of the dynamics internal to the business – a kind of ethical formalism – seeking to mask or obscure professional motivations within inspirational programmes for individual ennoblement and advancement. Primarily an individualistic ethos prepared to parody (in a business school sense) the 'symptoms' of an enlarged de-centred self-consciousness; in the service of professional recuperation. Under which increasing drive to centralize, metaphors and finally inept products of regionality competed – unfeasibly inadequately funded – for what was left of everyone's guilt. Something like this – possibly well-motivated – applies to Documenta11. If you take it seriously (and it's worth taking seriously), then there is no way that one should even consider looking at Cerith Wyn Evans in the same space – mental or physical – that one looks at E. Syvian (Rwandan genocide); because one's first obligation is to be pessimistic about the claims to seriousness of the one versus the overriding claim to attention of the other – which is not complimentary and not a different instance of the same thing.

By the way Matthew, did you notice the new

shrunken Untitled; made smaller to accommodate
all of Clare Bishop's interesting thoughts? Damp
Farquharson/Gillick accommodation – you
needed a wet suit to read the interview. Can that
be it now with Liam and the surprising
reappearance of the use of 'certain'?

"Magically sophisticated", that's nice – nice
underpinning of H. Potter – not extravagant.
MA

I don't think the Rwandan genocide film had
overriding claims for attention. You mention Liam
Gillick and Untitled. Well, did you read the
review at the back of the mag? It was a real
hatchet job from a slightly self-righteous
perspective ("I am really on the side of the left
wing guys and people on low wages etc.") – it
made me almost believe in Liam! More on Docu
11 tomorrow, drunk now. Actually earlier this
evening I was appalled at the memory of rantings
in my last Docu message.
MC

Actually I did. That's A. Scrivener who came up
to me in pub after your 'discussion' at Cubitt St.
and said: "What a wasted opportunity to really
tackle those critics!"

You should believe in Liam. Pretty and layered
work. He's just not the fabulous or diabolical
creature that some people imagine – and his work
is sometimes mildly prim and respectful – though
cunning and bright. It's that watery context that
makes the appearance of Tarka the Otter so
attractive. Otherwise it's just tedious to hear the

charge that he's – suave. We should all be so
bloody lucky, as Stanley Baker might say – circa
1970. Well … you're suave.

  Please … more … I'm not allowing any delusions
as to the quality of that clipped style – no hedging.
MA

Well I grant Liam his suaveness as a person and I
celebrate it – in fact I always have. In Art Crazy
Nation I grant him it and in his Unstapled
interview I was impressed by it too, once again. I
have very specific objections – the work is bullshit
and the cult of him among curators is bullshit.
The bullshitness is the trendiness and utter terror
of being thought unfashionable, and the lack of
any centre to all the cards piled against each
other. We know everything is constructed but so
what? It's only the same emptiness to say that as it
is to say that we know Picasso is a genius but so
what? In relation to Documenta the same
problem applies. Documenta might as well have
been a whole show by Liam, except for the one
or two works where there was some manual skill
or visual sophistication, which of course could
never have been mistaken for anything by Liam.
And I mean things like Louise Bourgeois's
dreadful Tracey Emin-a-likes, where Louise
showed a kind of work made of sewing that was a
Piglet (as in W. the Pooh) doll in the form of a
suffering ethnic type, in a spooky vitrine. So you
can see that I appreciate L's virtues quite clearly: at
least he doesn't do that Piglet stuff. Oh damn I
see what you mean now – that it's tedious to say
Liam is suave, not that it's important to notice

how suave he is. I must have been blind when I
thought I was reading your email. Plus I hardly
know myself what I was going on about re:
Piglet. Oh yes I remember, it was this head thing
by L. Bourgeois. I just re-read the review of Liam
by A. Scrivener and far from bad it seemed good.
That is very bad as in 'bad review' but good clear
critical thinking.
MC

And I think you're wrong: bullshit is not a specific
objection, or if it is it's a specific objection about a
genralization - bullshit. In the Unstabled
interview you found it attractive, again, to refer to
Gillick and to deplore something like his
unaestheticness or his lack of aesthetic
(obliterating the apparent dialogical or 'relational'
aspects of the work). I find Gillick's work
aesthetic, but I'm not sure that I feel like telling
you why. I don't like G. Rigden, for instance, but I
wouldn't be surprized to find out that he was
aesthetic and that you could point to those
features in his work that contained and registered
or even signalled or even better, *were* aesthetic -
and I bet that you would be right; it's just that in
any case (like 'Christian' or 'Samoan' or
'abandoned to liberals as a child in Notting Hill')
- 'aesthetic' isn't usually a non-trivial critical term.
Unless it is and it's yours and it means something
quite specific in which case show us your hand.
What does it mean? Specifically? I kind of feel
about this that you must be keeping an ace up
your sleeve, despite the fact that your sitting in the
dark bellowing "Trumps!" seems to be randomly

(though serially) motivated.

But I also think that you're abandoning, in caricaturing Gillick, some of the interesting ground. For instance: is he really such a child of international curatordom? I don't know what all the influences are, but I suspect that that international-curatorial sexpot caricature, from your Art Crazy Nation, is weak. And is that really such an homogenous grouping? Other than for the purposes of caricature? Wouldn't that grouping - at least in part - have been a product - not simply of course, or very much - of the influences of writers like you - at one point or another - even, or even especially if - you had been identified as a reactionary. And isn't the movement to marginalize yourself (not by working with me) by slumming it with allotment artists - just a bit cowardly? Couldn't one complain very easily that you are a bit glamorous and suave? Too? I'll be damned, I'm not sure I don't find you a bit aesthetic.

But Matthew; there is nothing in the middle of you. Just this saurian hot-pot Y. Shonibare critic being endlessly slobbered over by antiqued powdered RAs delighted by your horror of appearing fashionable ...
MA

By aesthetic I mean 'visually pleasing'. Liam's stuff is obviously fundamentally not visually pleasing. It has visual-pleasure absolute neutrality. Instead of pleasure it refers to visual pleasure as one of its many references, usually to pleasure in design. Therefore we don't have anything that's really a

thing, instead we are thrown back onto something else, we don't know what, exactly. Well obviously we do – it's a secret language (or open-secret) of internationally recognised (by art people) terms and phrases and mannerisms and so on. You could say this is the idea that the contemporary intellectual non-aesthete has of what abstract art is: a lot of secret language stuff about feeling and colour and brush strokes etc. But frankly we know without being Einstein that pleasure in brush strokes and so on has an objective element. And anyway it's not worth discussing whether it's objective or not as some kind of philosophical point. The real issue is that the Documenta/Liam world is concerned with things that are nothing except references: so they are trivial. It's just an error to take all that seriously. I think it's a failure – even if it's an understandable one – for you not to get Geoff Rigden. I do get Liam, and Documenta, and I object to them. You say something about caricaturing, and so on. But I think I caricature things because I'm looking for the argument, not as a way to avoid arguments.
MC

I don't find your explanation helpful. I'm prepared for the consequences of not getting Geoff Rigden – how many people can say as much? I still don't see anything consequential in your definition of 'aesthetic' – it's rather as if you were choosing to explain the concept 'circular' by drawing circles – neither do 'circles' appear to me nor does the circularity of your argument – who has the concept – occur to you. I don't have the concept that you are unable to articulate. Watch out giving me your concept - which I'm then able to articulate! What a mess! I would go around explaining why Geoff Rigden was good without even understanding him! Every time someone said "Aesthetic"!!

It's all very disgusting. I worry about all those illicit features of other peoples experiences that are suspiciously unquantifiable. But definitely true. And I want to decant the implacability of my own judgements and submit them, to you, for a prize. I hope that your pleasures do have an objective element - it's not weird to remind you that, in fact, I'm talking about your judgement.
MA

Well, Geoff Rigden is pleasing. Not all that pleasing actually, but still pleasing. That's what aesthetic means. Certain cars are more pleasingly designed than others. Certain paintings are more pleasingly painted. But the car language isn't a problem, whereas the painting language is a problem for the uninitiated, and a different kind of problem for the initiated. The first don't know what the hell's going on anyway, the second are corrupted by an inevitable knowing-too-much that comes with knowing anything beyond first base. The job of critics who are aesthetes is to describe what aesthetic pleasure is like, or what the aesthetic issues might be, etc, etc. It can be quite moving when they do that, because you don't often come across it. Not to philosophise about what 'aesthetic' is. Everyone who it's worth talking to about something 'aesthetic' already

knows what it is. It's not an opinion or arbitrary
or mystical to say that Rigden is aesthetic and
Gillick isn't. It's factually objectively scientifically
as well as poetically and subjectively true that
Liam's art is not visually pleasing but visually
neutral, or visually straining to even make it to
the lowest common denominator of democratic
visual pleasure. It's a visual parody of a set of ideas.
This sounds to some people like what Geoff
Rigden is - a visual parody of a set of special ideas
about the visual. But it's wrong to think that.
Liam is non-visual but not particularly idea-ish
either: he refers to ideas, just like he refers to the
visual and to the aesthetic (design aesthetic).
The difference with Rigden is that R. might refer
to a mastic tree (this is a logo theme in some of
his paintings). But it wouldn't matter if it were a
mushroom. The fact that it's not verifiable except
by asking him if it's a tree or a mushroom isn't
important. With Liam, asking him (Liam) is all-
important, because without that there's nothing
there. But his answers are not answers, they're just
hot air. I would never dream of taking anything
he said as something intended to be understood as
directly true and this is the case with the
Documenta curators too. If you ask Rigden
anything it's awful because he's a heavy drinker so
you just wouldn't anyway. Of course nothing is
really 'not aesthetic' but when I say that
something is - like Liam's exhibitions, or
Documenta - I feel anyone who would be in a
position to read me saying it (you know, socially
able to get any of this stuff at all) will know what
I mean. It's obvious I mean that stuff is a waste of

time, and the fact is, it is. I read this new book by
Hal Foster on the train the other day, and it's very
concise and even quite well written, for an art
book. Why do I have to look at a lot of nonsense
words by Liam? Or listen to a lot of simpering
teenage posturing by those crying curators? When
I can read a real book that's written by someone
(HF) who's only fault is to be a bit dour and self-
righteous? But who is prepared to make an effort
and put the hours in, and hone the paragraphs a
bit, and who actually has something informed and
clear to say about design and architecture and
society and modernity and the middle class? I'm
not even all that interested in those issues anyway.
But if I was I certainly would want to hear
something about it that someone actually meant;
than have to get the (non) message by mystical
telepathy by looking at a lot of flabby open-ended
visually mild allegories.
MC

And I agree with you about a lot of this. It's not
quite right though to dismiss as 'philosophical' a
complaint just about the vagueness of your
terminology; funnily enough I'm prepared to
accept that the 'aesthetic' is what you refer to as
your own (Matthew Colling's) objectively
pleasing experiences under further conditions of
specificity as described by you - which, I guess,
for a philosopher, would probably not be
something to have a go at. But also I think it's
right to attach this to your judgement, which
might refer to a bedrock without chipping up bits
of mineral and offering them for analysis. Actually,

what I think is really interesting is the warrant that you have. Which is to interpret statutes put down by Society. A society somewhat like a cross between the old-West and a market-town in olde-Bedfordshire awaiting the arrival of the Assizes. Here comes Sheriff/hanging-judge J.P. Collings. All you pesky indians/bog-oirish go back to your reserves/squalid fever-infested Gaelic hovels and drink yourselves to a pathetic end – and no more interviews. Or magic.

Actually (again?), I thought your writing about Milton Keynes show was a nice mix of arch and philosophically illuminating – obviously much more so than anything in Documenta catalogue. Where there was an attempt to determine some issues in a recognizably philosophical – other than just thoughtful – context. So of course some (not all) of the writing, like the art, a titchy bit provoking – but anyone would agree with you a bit or a lot; but of course not about specific instances: Flintstones – which is, again of course, where the argument narrows and bottlenecks and becomes non-platitudinous. Where for instance I say – no, I don't agree with you; I liked G. Gabellone for this or that quite specific reason – e.g. reductive (or other equivalent to 'elegant') in relation to known dichotomies, whereas I thought Shonibare was a bit 'Mousetrap', which I would also understand – under certain dormitory conditions – might have some charm. And then also even some of the writing was better than some other bits of writing – actually (Tsssk), S. Maharaj is good in that little short catalogue – but listen to me! There I go confidently finding comfortable qualities on the basis of a truncation into my own language of a writer whose first language must be ... English.

But I'm not confident that I understand you although I think that you are right to produce the warrant for the 'rightness' of your opinion and I admire that it is consistent with a non-metaphysical view of everybody else's productions where they conflict with your own, experienced and circuited, judgements.
MA

Have to finish writing intro to John Moores exhibition but will reply later. Still can't remember what Gabbeone did - describe it in detail for me, in objective way. I do have a little Documenta catalogue actually but I can't bring myself to dig it out.
MC

What I think is: That they take a narrowness, an established set of commonplaces relating to potentialities - between photography and sculpture and installation - and discount accordingly and in a way that is unusually generous and revelatory. A big reward for a tight idea that's close - in affect - to recovering something from an unpromising situation.
MA

Sorry, my explanation not very convincing - rushed. Also maybe should stick to works we both know?
MA

Well OK but I still don't know what they are. In
any case they sound horrible. But I'll look them
up. What's supposed to be the idea of them?
MC

According to catalogue: 'Gabellone's photographic
series of artificial flowers … images of blue
polystyrene flower sculptures'. But less 'value-free'
– 'The sculptural experience is replaced by the
photograph, which has become a permanent, yet
incomplete duplicate of the sculpture'. But give it
up. Of course I don't have any objective descriptions
of works to offer – they wouldn't be descriptions.
And that's just purely a silly idea, that you want
the facts 'in-the-case'. And no one is interested.
I could tell you where these works were located
within the building – but I'm not even sure that
that would be this weird thing that you are
demanding – 'objective'. I have descriptions and
opinions and they are not like Siamese twins and
you can't do a sponsored run and raise money to
get them separated.
  And anyway – I'm not your dog that you can
command to bring you facts.
  So, I'm not a dog or a Siamese twin or a sieve to
take out the rocks; and, if anyone's translating me
back into the Queen's English – it's not you you
big beefeater. With your weird anachronisms.
And ravens.
  By the way – good luck with John Moores.
MA

So, looking back: it seems as if our exchange has
been a trot round the bounds of your property –

checking the fences for incursions, with you on 16 hands of glossy pie-bald thoroughbred and me muddily taking notes. And as you've been demanding a non-philosophical context, in fact – a domestic context (with the regularities just as you like them), in which to become bellicose about your 'aesthetic' – especially on damp evenings when the fire won't draw properly; and then thunder at the staff for not supplying fresh young 'stuff' (just as you like it) – I feel like taking sides with Emma – you brute.

In fact, more specifically, it seems to me that you are prepared to philosophize furiously and then send me off on a search across a flattened globe – curling in the damp – for correspondingly uni-dimensional facts. Like Hypogriffs (documentagriffs) – facts that derive their factual basis in your sherry-soaked Uncle Tobyish brain. As you crash and grumble and huff and swash your way about your dusty molecularized library with tattered bits of paper that name ancient enemies – Liamus Gillickus – etc. etc. – stuck to your head with horsey-glue. Occasionally swiping a token curly-haired-artist's head mounted at a precarious angle on the wall – "Damn you all why won't you talk to me – you jesuitical (swoosh, swipe) johnny-come-latelies (swish, whip) – Aesthetic I tell ye, AESTHETIC an' damn the whole unholy foringer caboodle of ye!"

Dong … Gerdong … Gerdong. "Damn! Who's that at the door? – well bless my socks – it's young Prince Charlesworth! Come in, come in – you know you're always welcome at Holloway House, sit yourself down Sir and tell me all about the big

old world – whats-a-foot? Have they got rid of that Thatcher women yet? How's Hal? Nobody tells me anything. I don't get out you know – it's this damn aesthetic leg of mine..."
MA

Maggie tells me that that was rude – just rude. So I'm sorry. Emma appeared in that context just because her name resonated. Probably triggered by Charlesworth also linking Foster with Greenberg. Tooth surgery awaits …
MA

Sorry I haven't replied sooner. It's not that I'm sulking. I was distracted by John Moores, had to write an essay for it. Essay was very good. Hope you will come to the opening on 12th September. I didn't think you were rude. I just bought frieze, it's full of articles about Documenta, plus ones about children's books, manatees, designer shelving and airlines, and I'm not being satirical. I looked up your guy in the Documenta catalogue and read the passage on him. There was a picture of an earlier work which was an exercise in strength and weakness – I don't know if you've got the same catalogue? The pic shows a kitsch photo of some flamingos, which is presented in a kind of truth-to-materials referring sculpture, with the sculpture acting as a frame for the photo-image. So you see something that's phoney contextualised by something 'true'. It seemed a very efficient work about concerns that seem academic to me. In the writing about him there was a sentence or two about the polystyrene

flowers photos you mention, which made them
seem even worse than the flamingos. But they
could be good inadvertently, and maybe this is the
one work by this guy that is good. Anyway I'm
going to read those articles in frieze now and
then get back to you.
MC

Hi, got sidetracked from absorbing frieze because
read JJ Charlesworth on formalism in Art
Monthly. Plus saw there was an article in Texte
Zur Kunst (do you know it?) from a year ago or
so, complaining about me, by Merlin Carpenter.
But couldn't understand it because can't speak
German; so had to find professional translator,
who it turns out wants £150 for the job - so
foolishly hired him; now I'm waiting for the text
to arrive, so I can fume about it.
MC

Just finished Thomas McEvilley on Documenta.
Very impressed by his facts and figures on gender
representation and white vs. non-white etc;
thought he must have been motivated by jealousy,
since I can't imagine anyone putting such an
effort into the maths unless they had an axe to
grind. After all, he helped invent this area (post-
colonial art) with that mag he used to edit (was it
called Contemporanea?) and his row with MoMA
New York over the Primitivism show in the 80s,
conducted in the letters page of Artforum. (But
which folded because it was so boring, I guess –
that mag of his, I mean.) (Sorry about brackets
being confusing. I can't remember the real reason.

I'm sure it wasn't because it was boring. I don't
know. Are we still aiming to publish this stuff? I
think we should!) Anyway, he also did an
admirable summing up of the theme of Doc 11.
And of the whole development of post–colonial
type shows of the last 30 years; and pointed out
that although this stuff has been in the air for all
this time, this is the first time it's actually been
nailed down as the big issue. And he described a
bit of the press conference, which I had found so
dire, because of the appalling tedious mannerist
affectedness of the speakers, which made me want
to shake them; and then described each of the
four main bits of the show. All the way through
the descriptions I must admit I kind of wondered
if there weren't little tiny cracks of irony or
distance. These were signalled to me in the use of
words like 'droned' in the context of the sound of
voices in conceptual art films, and 'worthy' in the
context of practically every artist in the show.
But it turned out no, he really did think it was all
top stuff. He genuinely thought it was authentic
art that really was about 'knowledge-production'
as one of the greatest brains on the curator-panel
put it. And not feeble pseudo nonsense made for
Biennalles (even though in fact 70 per cent of it
was - as McE pointed out, using his calculator -
literally made for this Documenta). He mentions
your guy, saying he's the youngest at 29, while the
average age of the exhibitors is 52 (I think). One
thing I did get from the article, although I don't
know if he meant to convey it, was the following.
The idea that I think I'm usually going on about
myself all the time, but maybe I never put it

clearly, that the show - and in fact art now at this
moment - was all about meaning and significance.
That is, a lot of Documenta is random typing. Or
random non-edited-looking filming. The latter is
about non-significance in the same kind of way as
the former. While what isn't either of those is
about piling up absurdly cliched ideas of
significance, which in reality expresses the
opposite of significance.
MC

I know you wouldn't sulk. I was a bit provoked by
being treated like a research assistant. And I don't
feel like agreeing with you. Being insulted in
German probably does mean something - don't
you think?
I think that you've given up too much high-
ground to your Documenta 'set'. I don't think
that it is your parody and I also think that, right
now, parodying worthiness or post-colonialism is
counter-productive - because it already seems a
familiar parody. Try parodying worthlessness.
I think it's worth following the textual grain of
any specific work - in order, of course, to view
works' 'insertion' into issues, even dumb issues.
But sometimes artists handle, or outflank or
disturb generative criteria; specifically. So I
nominate an artist and a whole lot of spittle-
flecked disparagement-machinery grinds into
motion and I get lobbed at by fast and slow
missiles.
But what does seem interesting is that you want
to mediate this all through others' writings -
which, kind of, suits me. What is it? In order to

open yourself up you need to go through the
purple patches and dark hues and mystic
dogmatic phrases of someone else? Your own
psychological miracle, a projected midget-infested
Triassic swamp is what you get - you're going to
have to go veiled and swishy-swiping all day.
I think this subject-matter is ripe with pitfalls -
even though I don't think of you as 'the unwary'.
MA

Gabellone doesn't make me furious. I see his
work, at least from the Documenta catalogue pic
and text, as obvious. It's about issues that are not
issues; they're for the sake of producing this work.
The work's content is empty and anyone can see
that. The thing hasn't got any presence, it's not a
serious thing. It hasn't got any shape to it. It's got
association-textures. You see the texture, you
associate it with something - like the non-shape
sculptures in 'Early One Morning' (the exhibition
at the Whitechapel at the moment, not the Caro
sculpture of 1962 or whenever, which of course
does have a shape. Even if it comes from a time
when 'shape' was some kind of voodoo issue for
articles in Studio International). You're even told in
advance what to associate. The weakness of the
little text about Gabellone isn't the problem. The
problem is the weakness of the work. 'Weak' in
this case means silly, thin and predictable. These
are the words that apply to Documenta as a
whole. If you read the McEvilley article you will
see that I'm not entirely parodying. He wants to
say that these things in Documenta are actually
'worthy' and that's the important part of his article.

Whereas what I saw were contemporary cliches of worthiness, so of course I say they're not worthy, they're objectionable. It's positively good actually not to have issues and meaning when both have become so ridiculous. Pettibon is a relief because there aren't any issues worth talking about in his shows. Comic style drawing and inking, plagiarised text-fragments put into mismatched comic strip scenes, rough latter-day Abstract Expressionist-parody (or painterly pop) spatters and drips on wall, pages ripped and torn, imagery stuck any old how on walls, and general feel of visual niceness – what else? War, death, aggression, masculinity, Batman, Superman, Green Lantern, homosexual Sgt. Furys indebted to Tom o' Finland, etc. These are all nothingnesses in a way, or very-littlenesses. Not because of the terms of the comedy way in which they're now part of art, but because of the fact that they *are* part of art – they are just some new cliches that all curators are familiar with. But the fact is there's some relief when someone does it well. Those drips are already empty to begin with and you don't have to scratch your head to find some rhizomes in Delueze with which to fill them up. However long it took for Pettibon to whack all that stuff on the walls (a day or an hour or half an hour) that was time well spent. But however many months and years it takes On Kawara's out of work actors to announce all the numbers up to a million, well, that will never match the tedium of having to look at the pages of Ecke Bonk's dictionary. Or Hanne Darboven's counting one to ten in Arabic.
MC

Our last emails crossed so I'm not sure if they still
fit? I suppose Pettibon is in the show because of
the category of trendy marginality, yes. Same as L.
Bourgeois I suppose. And L. Golub because he
used to paint those scenes of torturers in South
America, for earlier Biennales and art fairs etc.. I
saw a film by Pettibon once about Jim Morrison,
where Morrison was a still-surviving alcoholic,
age about mid 50s, going to AA meetings to pick
up girls. It seemed a masterpiece! Those Golubs
and Bourgeoises were terrible. McEvilley - sorry
to keep mentioning him - didn't seem to actually
see the Golubs I saw: they were incredibly flabby,
but McE seemed to think it summed up G's
greatness and apropo-ness to say he did them
with a 'meat cleaver'. McE actually thought it
was some kind of blow against oppression that
Golub shaved off the paint surface using a meat
cleaver. I suppose because 'surfaces' in paint are
like expensive cakes or pastries that only the cruel
people of this world can afford. He described
Glen Ligon's paintings as 'conceptual' but in fact
they were the usual light silly inadvertent (because
empty but assuming itself to be profound)
formalism that you see everywhere, and in pages
of Artforum and frieze. It's not the formalism I
object to but the lightness. Pettibon is very visual.
I don't object to his adolescent-ism, because it's
the vehicle not the content. And in the bits
where it is the content it's quite funny. It makes
sense to have him in the Documenta because of
terrorists, I suppose, not just marginality. He has a
lot of cartoons about comic strip terrorist types
and Twin Towers fears. I mean, terrorists are

definitively marginal, while Pettibon is
mainstream and only pseudo-marginal, or
'marginal'. But the sudden rise of terrorists as
material for mainstream 'meaning-production' is
irrelevant to whether Pettibon's any good. In
general, the Documenta theme isn't irrelevant, it's
fine of course. But I can't help it if the art's a bit
rough - the artists shouldn't copy what their
superiors tell them to do. They shouldn't have
superiors. After all (re: McEvilley's point that the
age average is quite high) what is advanced age
for, but to learn to think for yourself?
MC

Well Matthew - I think that you are unfreezing a
little, although I think that there is still something
cryogenic about your tendency to specify an artist
and describe his or her work and then use that
description to 'name' that work. So that context
becomes like a riddle of all the adding-up of or
acting-out of bits of your descriptions - like
naughty Pokemon come to life. You've got away
with it before, i.e. all the way through the
Nineties, when your descriptions were often
simply better than the British art that you
described; and that's not saying *such* a damning
thing - though when it fails it leaves your
descriptions unsupported - like my back tooth
until yesterday. Or increasingly supported by
fillings. Or American artists. Or a backtracking
respect for that stone-washed classicist McEvilley.
Or some sudden rather acute observations on
Pettibon. Linked to some timely remarks on
terrorism. (Mine just fall out).

Here's a quote for you from Baumgarten:

'Suppose we observe someone in a state of
wonder at something, for example,
an artfully constructed implement of war. If we
want to check his wonder, we can ask him
whether he has not seen the same thing even
more artfully constructed at Berlin or Dresden. If
he remembers it, his wonder decreases.'

But I don't see any differences in Documenta11:
a differently deflated and blown-up transaction of
European self-consciousness. Wonderingly,
irritatingly disassociated with reality – other than
that type of 'reality', the spectre of The Globe as
an Idea. Chomsky, rather than Said or Spivak,
authoring the unacknowledged type which has at
its core; a belief in the universal – even universal
disjunction, as it engages in an almost militaristic
deployment of universalizations.
There is a conflict between professional
individualism, totalizing or authoritarian
individuation and radical preoccupations at the
specific level of the show. The conflict between
that confidence in structurally determining or
prescribing and then erasing or transcending that
humanistic motivation is the kind of problem
(where all those resulting determinations really
ought to be seen as devices) planted by, and then
faced by, organizers. Drably, at a critical level, the
answer would be to be insistently local and
specific; in that sense 'anti-theoretical'. Which is a
theoretical as well as an oblivious response and
one I think you've exercised with skill, before.

The danger is in appearing to be an
unreconstructed formalist from the point of view
of being that person - naturally. As if there were
no urbane alternative to the slurred and rabbit-
eared absolutist projections of the retreat into
'otherness'.
  And reality is full of more convincing teenagers
than Pettibon as well as horrific and shocking
terrors in Rwanda. To which you may have the
right to respond - "of course".
MA

You have to learn to be a formalist and therefore
you can't be an unreconstructed one or a natural
one. But I think the intensity of the formalism is
the point; all the Documenta artists are formalists,
it's just that I object to them being feeble ones.
MC

But some people might prefer not. I think that
your exfoliations have left the trees still happily
fruiting. I enjoyed Documenta11. I didn't much
like any of the bigger name stuff.
  I liked Gabellone, Dominique Gonzalez-
Foerster, Le Groupe Amos, Huit Facettes, Igloolik
Isuma, Alfredo Jaar, Johan van der Keuken,
Olumuyiwa Olamide Osifuye, Manfred Pernice,
Adrian Piper, Gilles Saussier, Lorna Simpson, Eyal
Sivan, Yan Fudong - probably Fudong and
Osifuye and Sivan most.
  I would have liked almost exactly one fifth of
the Sekula stuff. But you are right - not much in
there to compare with Gillick. Maybe the cutest
little Darboven film. They could have used one or

two aerial McFlurries. At least something a bit
sweeter and brighter with a sense of it's own
glossy flanks.
 You do know don't you – that you are
recalcitrant? Like one nice piece of colour
bumping-up against another. But not dead-eyed,
not a still-life, very much alive and kicking.
Bruisingly dashing in a non-lop-eared way.
MA

I can't think of anything else. I totally didn't enjoy
Documenta. The works I didn't find hateful were
no compensation for the feeling of total
unenjoyment I mostly had.
MC

Matthew Arnatt & Matthew Collings.
Thanks to Dustin Ericksen.